A LITTLE
WEST COUNTRY
Cookbook

Rosa Mashiter
Illustrated by Linda Smith

Appletree Press

First published in 1996 by
The Appletree Press Ltd.
19-21 Alfred Street, Belfast BT2 8DL
Tel. +44 232 243074 Fax +44 232 246756
Copyright © 1996 The Appletree Press Ltd.
Printed in the U.A.E. All rights reserved.
no part of this publication may be reproduced or
transmitted in any form or by any means, electronic or
mechanical, photocopying, recording or any information
and retrieval system, without permission in writing from
The Appletree Press Ltd.

A Little West Country Cookbook

A catalogue record for this book is available in
The British Library.

ISBN 0-86281-571-1

9 8 7 6 5 4 3 2 1

A Note on Measures

All spoon measurements are level rather than
heaped. Recipes are for four unless
otherwise indicated.

The West Country enjoys the mildest climate in England and has access to a wonderful variety of natural ingredients. Agriculture in one form or another is the backbone of the economy. Farms raise cattle, sheep, pigs and chickens. Dairy cattle which graze on the rich green pastures of the West Country provide exceptionally rich milk which is ideal for the traditional thick cream and for the famous cheeses of the area like Cheddar, Curworthy, and Cornish Yarg. There's plenty of game to be had from the woods, and the rivers offer some of the best tasting salmon and trout. Hedgerows are thick with wild fruit, sloes and plump, glistening blackberries, and wild field mushrooms are never hard to find. The seas that surround much of this region are warmed by the Gulf Stream and produce an abundance of shellfish like crab and lobster and a wonderful variety of flat and deep sea fish. West Country food has a richness of flavour all of its own - even the most humble of dishes are to be relished.

Raw Tattie Fry

There are not many regional breakfast dishes, but Raw Tattie Fry is pure West Country and very popular. If the bacon is not used it is known as Potato Jowdle.

1 oz (25g) lard
6 rashers bacon, rinds removed
1 large onion, peeled and thinly sliced
4 large potatoes, peeled and very thinly sliced
Salt and freshly ground black pepper
½ pint (300ml) water
1 tbsp (15ml) oil
4 eggs

Melt half the lard in a large heavy-bottomed frying pan and cook the bacon until the fat is starting to crisp. Add the onion and the rest of the lard if needed. Cook until the onion has softened but not browned, then add the potato slices, season with salt and black pepper and pour in the water. Cover and simmer gently for about 30 minutes by which time the potatoes should be cooked. Remove the lid for the last ten minutes to enable the potatoes to crisp up on top. Heat the oil in a frying pan, and fry the eggs until set. Divide the potato mixture onto four separate plates and top each serving with a fried egg.

Kettle Broth

This simple but extremely effective soup used to be prepared for farm workers, the contents of the pot reflecting the fortunes of the farmer. In lean times it might just be some leek tops, roughly chopped, combined with stale bread spread with dripping, all soaked in boiling water. Whatever the contents the soup was always sprinkled with edible marigold petals believed to prevent many minor ailments. The name originates from the large iron cauldron known as a "kettle" in which the soup was prepared.

2 oz (50g) dripping
1 large onion, peeled and chopped
2 fat leeks, washed and thinly sliced
3 slices of bread, crusts removed
2 pints (1.2 litre) chicken stock
Salt and freshly ground black pepper
½ pint (300ml) milk

Heat the dripping in a large saucepan and cook the onions and leeks until soft and transparent. Add the bread and stock, bring to the boil, season, lower the heat and simmer for 30-40 minutes. Puree the soup in a food processor and return to a clean pan. Add the milk and heat through, without boiling. Scatter some edible marigold petals on top of each bowl.

Baked Sole with Prawn and Parsley Butter

There is a great variety of fish and shellfish around the shores and seas of the South West. Megrim sole is peculiar to the seas in this region but lemon sole or even plaice can be used.

4 sole fillets, skinned
Pinch of white pepper
1 tbsp (15ml) lemon juice
2 tbsp (30ml) fresh breadcrumbs
1 tbsp (15ml) grated Parmesan cheese
2 oz (50g) butter
1 clove garlic crushed
1 tbsp (15ml) finely chopped fresh parsley
2 oz (50g) peeled prawns, finely chopped

Season the fillets with pepper and lemon juice, roll up neatly and place in a lightly greased ovenproof dish. Mix the breadcrumbs and cheese together and sprinkle over the fish, cover with foil and bake at 190°C, 375°F, gas mark 5 for about 20 minutes. Meanwhile soften the butter and put into a food processor together with the garlic, parsley and prawns. Blend well, form into a roll on a piece of foil, refrigerate to firm. Just before serving the fillets top each one with a generous slice of the savoury butter.

Crab Cakes

Crabs from this region are usually large and succulent, and though you can buy them whole, it is easier for this recipe just to buy the small quantity of crabmeat required from your fishmonger. Delicious served for lunch or dinner with a home-made tomato sauce.

1½ lbs (675g) peeled potatoes
½ pint (300ml) milk
2 eggs, hard boiled
8 oz (225g) mix of white and brown crabmeat
2 tsp (10ml) wholegrain mustard
2 tbsp (30ml) chopped fresh parsley
Salt and freshly ground black pepper
3 tbsp (45ml) flour
4 tbsp (60ml) oil

Cook the potatoes until tender, drain and mash with enough milk for a firm mixture. Finely chop the hard-boiled eggs and fold into the potato mixture together with the crab, mustard and parsley then season well. Shape the mixture into eight round, flat cakes. Spread the flour on the plate, season with salt and black pepper and press the cakes into the flour to coat, dusting away any excess. Heat the oil in a frying pan and cook the crab cakes gently, in two batches, for 3-5 minutes on each side until golden. Drain on kitchen paper.

Grilled Tamar Salmon

The river Tamar, which has its source high on the moors in Devon, separates the counties of Devon and Cornwall and is home to some of the best salmon in the British Isles.

Salt and freshly ground black pepper
4 salmon cutlets, about ½ inch (1cm) thick
4 oz (100g) butter
½ tsp (2.5ml) lemon juice
2 tbsp (30ml) finely chopped fresh parsley

Lightly season the salmon cutlets and place on a rack in a grill pan. Melt half the butter and brush some over the salmon. Grill under a medium high heat for about 5 minutes. Turn the steaks over and brush with a little more melted butter and cook for a further 3 minutes. Transfer the steaks to a hot serving dish and keep warm. Pour the juices from the grill pan into a small saucepan, add the remaining butter and heat until it has melted. Stir in the lemon juice and parsley, season, and pour over the steaks. Serve with some tiny Cornish new potatoes.

Smoked Mackerel Pate

Mackerel is one of the biggest catches off the West Country coast, and much of it is smoked locally giving it a very individual flavour.

1 small onion
1 clove garlic
4 oz (100g) butter
8oz (225g) smoked mackerel, with skin and bones removed
Juice of ½ lemon
¼ pint (150ml) double cream
Freshly ground black pepper
Pinch of ground mace
Pinch of cayenne pepper

Peel and finely chop the onion. Peel and crush the garlic. Heat half the butter in a saucepan and cook the onion and garlic, over a gentle heat, until the onion is soft and transparent. Put the flaked fish, onion and garlic with cooking juices and the remaining butter in a food processor and blend until smooth. Add the lemon juice and cream, season with freshly ground black pepper and the spices and blend again. Pack into small pots and chill until firm. Serve with hot buttered toast or crusty brown bread.

Pheasant Pie

Game is extremely popular in the West Country, and there is never a shortage of pheasants during the shooting season.

1 brace pheasants, plucked, drawn and trussed
8 rashers of streaky bacon with the rinds removed
4 large leeks, thinly sliced
1 large cooking apple, peeled, cored and diced
2 oz (50g) butter
2 oz (50g) flour
1 pint (600ml) good stock
1 tbsp (15ml) dried tarragon
Salt and freshly ground black pepper
1 x 13 oz (350g) packet frozen puff pastry, thawed
1 small egg, beaten

Brush the pheasants with a little oil and roast at 190°C, 375°F, gas mark 5 for 45 minutes. Remove from the oven and when cool enough strip off the meat and cut into bite size pieces. Cut each rasher of bacon in half and shape into small rolls. Spread the leeks in a large pie dish, cover with the pheasant, bacon rolls and diced apple. Melt the butter in a saucepan and stir in the flour. Over a medium high heat gradually stir in the stock and bring to the boil. The sauce should be thick and smooth. Stir in the tarragon and season. Pour the sauce over the ingredients in the dish. Roll out the pastry and use to make a lid, sealing off the edges well, brush with beaten egg and bake for 45 minutes at 190°C, 375°F, gas mark 5.

Devonshire Lamb with Peas

Wherever you go in the West Country you will see sheep: a valuable part of the economy of the region, both for food and for their wool. This recipe makes a full and nourishing meal.

1 oz (25ml) oil
8 lamb chops
1 lb (450g) fresh peas
1 onion, finely chopped
2 tsp (10ml) sugar
1 tbsp (15ml) fresh mint, finely chopped
½ pint (300ml) stock
Salt and freshly ground black pepper
1½ lbs (675g) potatoes, cooked and mashed
2 tbsp (30ml) Cheddar cheese, grated

Heat the oil in a frying pan and brown the chops, then place in a large pie dish. Mix the peas, onion, sugar and mint together, season with salt and black pepper and add to the dish. Cover with foil and bake at 180°C, 350°F, gas mark 4 for one hour. Remove from oven and take off foil. Pile the mashed potato on top, sprinkle over the grated cheese and return to the oven for a further 30 minutes.

Cornish Under Roast

A real farmhouse dish, making good use of the more inexpensive cuts of meat.

Flour to coat
Salt and freshly ground black pepper
1 lb (450g) shin beef, trimmed and cubed
8 oz (225g) kidney, trimmed and roughly chopped
2 tbsp (30ml) oil
1 medium onion, peeled and thinly sliced
2 carrots, peeled and sliced
1 pint (600ml) beef stock
1 lb (450g) potatoes, peeled and thickly sliced

Season a little flour with salt and black pepper and use to coat the meat cubes and kidney. Heat the oil in a flameproof casserole dish, add the meat and brown all over. Remove with a slotted spoon. Add the onion and carrots to the dish and cook until the onion has started to soften. Return the meat to the dish and pour over the stock. Bring to the boil, cover and simmer for 30 minutes. Place the potatoes on top of the dish, and put in a preheated oven, uncovered, at 170°C, 325°F, gas mark 3 for 2 hours. The top of the potatoes should be crisp and golden.

Beef in Cider

Cider making first came to the West Country in the thirteenth century and the inclusion of cider brings a special local flavour to many dishes.

1 onion, peeled and roughly chopped
2 carrots, cut into chunks
3 lbs (1.5kg) salted brisket of beef
1 tbsp (5ml) mixed herbs
1 tsp (5ml) mixed herbs
10 black peppercorns
10 cloves
1 tsp (5ml) ground allspice
Salt and freshly ground black pepper
1 pint (600ml) dry cider
1 pint (600ml) hot beef stock

Place the onion and carrots in the bottom of a large heavy casserole dish (a cast iron one is ideal for this dish) and place the meat on top. Sprinkle the herbs and spices over the beef, season, and pour over the cider and hot beef stock. Cover the dish tightly (use two layers of foil and then the lid) and cook at 130°C, 250°F, gas mark 1 for about 4 hours. Remove the dish from the oven and leave the meat to cool in it overnight. Transfer the meat to a dish into which it just fits, put a weighted plate on top and leave in a cool place for 24 hours. The beef should be served very thinly sliced accompanied by a selection of pickles and salads.

Sausages in Cider

It was the Romans who first introduced the sausage to Britain - fresh, dried and smoked - and we have been a nation of sausage eaters ever since. In the West Country nearly all local butchers make their own varieties offering a remarkable range of flavours and ingredients.

2 large onions, peeled and thinly sliced
1 lb (450g) thick pork sausages
1 tbsp (15ml) coarse grain mustard
1 tsp (5ml) mixed herbs
Salt and freshly ground black pepper
½ pint (300ml) dry cider

Arrange the sliced onions in the bottom of an ovenproof dish. Place the sausages on top and cook for 10 minutes in a hot oven at 220°C, 425°F, gas mark 7. Mix the mustard, herbs and seasoning with a little of the cider and then blend in the remaining cider and pour this mixture over the sausages. Lower the oven to 190°C, 375°F, gas mark 5) and continue cooking for a further 25-30 minutes. Serve with chunks of crusty bread.

Wiltshire Gammon

Wiltshire is renowned for its bacon and ham, both of which can be bought smoked or unsmoked. At one time it was essential to soak bacon overnight to remove the excess salt from the brine curing, but these days it is generally not necessary.

2 lb (900g) Wiltshire gammon joint
1 small onion stuck with 4 cloves
1 bay leaf
3 tbsp (45ml) Dijon mustard
1 tbsp (15ml) soft dark brown sugar
2 oz (50g) fresh breadcrumbs
1 small egg, beaten

Place the gammon in cold water and bring to the boil. Drain and place in fresh cold water to cover, add the onion and the bay leaf. Bring to the boil, reduce the heat and simmer for 20 minutes per pound (450g). Prepare the topping mixture by mixing all the dry ingredients together and binding them with the beaten egg. Remove the gammon from the cooking liquid and place in a roasting tin. Allow to cool slightly then using a sharp knife cut off the rind. Score the fat in a criss-cross diagonal pattern and spread the mustard topping on the surface. Cook in a hot oven at 200°C, 400°F, gas mark 6 for 15 minutes when the top should be crusty and golden. Serve hot with fresh seasonal vegetables or cold with a selection of pickles and chutneys.

Leek (Likky) Pie

At one time this pie would not have contained any meat and would have been eaten during Lent to provide sustenance.

4 oz (100g) streaky bacon, rinds removed
6 leeks, washed and cut into 1 inch (2.5cm) lengths
¼ pint (150ml) chicken stock
1 bay leaf
12oz (340g) shortcrust pastry
1 small egg, beaten

Roughly chop the bacon and fry in a non-stick pan without any additional fat until just crisping. Add the leeks and cook, tossing lightly, for 2 - 3 minutes. Pour in just sufficient stock to cover, add the bay leaf, and simmer for 15 minutes. Remove from the heat and pour away most of the liquid. Allow the leek and bacon mixture to cool. Roll out the pastry into two circles to fit a shallow pie dish or pie plate, and line the dish with a pastry circle. Spread the leek and bacon mixture on top, brush around the pastry edge of the pie with water and place the remaining pastry circle on top, sealing the edges well. Make a small slit in the centre of the pie, brush with beaten egg and cook for 40 minutes at 190°C, 375°F, gas mark 5.

Squab Pie

This pie used to be made with plump young pigeons (otherwise known as squabs), but over the years with the difficulty of obtaining these birds other meats have been substituted which taste just as good.

4 oz (100g) margarine
8 oz (225g) plain flour
1 lb (450g) neck fillet of lamb, sliced
1 lb (450g) onions, peeled and thinly sliced
1 cooking apple, peeled, cored and diced
½ tsp (2.5ml) ground allspice
Salt and freshly ground black pepper
¼ pint (150ml) chicken stock
1 small egg, beaten

In a mixing bowl rub the fat into the flour with your fingertips until the mixture resembles fine breadcrumbs adding sufficient cold water for a firm dough. Layer the lamb, onions and apple into a small dish, seasoning each layer with allspice, salt and black pepper. Pour over the stock. Roll out the pastry on a lightly-floured board and use to cover the pie, dampening the edge of the dish so that the pastry adheres. Decorate with pastry trimmings. Brush with beaten egg and bake for 20 minutes at 200°C, 400°F, gas mark 6 then lower the heat to 180°C, 350°F, gas mark 4 for a further hour. Cover the pastry with a sheet of greaseproof paper if it starts to over brown.

Pepper Pot

This spicy dish is a cross between a stew and a soup. It first became popular in the West Country in the eighteenth century, when traders brought their exotic cargoes from the New World into the port of Bristol. The writer Thomas Brown described it at that time as "the most delicate palate-scorching concoction called pepper pot".

2 lbs (900g) lean diced leg of lamb
8 oz (225g) back bacon, diced
3 onions, peeled and finely chopped
2 fresh chilli peppers, deseeded
2 green peppers, deseeded and sliced
1 tbsp (15ml) finely chopped thyme
1 tsp (5ml) cayenne pepper
1 tsp (5ml) paprika
Salt and peppercorns
8 oz (225g) cabbage, very finely shredded
4 oz (100g) shelled prawns, roughly chopped

Serves 8

Put the lamb, bacon and onions in a large saucepan with 3 pints (1.8 litres) cold water. Add the chillies, green peppers, thyme, cayenne pepper, paprika, peppercorns and salt. Bring to the boil, cover and simmer over a low heat for about 2 hours. Add the cabbage and cook for a further 20 minutes. Add the prawns and cook for a further 5 minutes only. Serve in large soup bowls accompanied by plain boiled rice.

West Country Potatoes

A delicious combination of potatoes, leeks, mature Cheddar cheese and ham, this dish is evocative of all that is good in local produce.

2 tbsp (30ml) oil
2 medium leeks, trimmed, cleaned and thinly sliced
4 medium potatoes, peeled and thinly sliced
6 oz (170g) gammon ham, minced and finely chopped
Salt and freshly ground black pepper
4 tbsp (60ml) chicken stock
1½ oz (40g) mature Cheddar cheese, grated
Pinch of ground nutmeg

Heat the oil in a frying pan, add the leeks and cook over a low heat, stirring, until the leeks are soft. Arrange a layer of potatoes at the bottom of a lightly-greased baking dish, cover with a layer of leeks, a scattering of minced ham and season with salt and pepper. Continue layering up the dish, finishing with potatoes. Add the stock. Sprinkle over the cheese and a generous pinch of ground nutmeg. Bake for about an hour at 180°C, 350°F, gas mark 4 until the top is golden brown and the potatoes, when tested with a knife, are tender.

Dorset Apple Cake

This recipe comes from Dorset but similar apple cakes can be found throughout the West Country. It is a good way of using up windfall apples.

4 oz (100g) butter or margarine
8 oz (225g) self-raising flour
8 oz (225g) cooking apples, peeled, cored and grated
4 oz (100g) caster sugar
2 oz (50g) sultanas
1 egg, beaten

In a large mixing bowl rub the butter into the flour, using the fingertips until the mixture resembles fine breadcrumbs. Stir in the grated apples, sugar and sultanas. Add the beaten egg and mix to a firm dough. Transfer to a lightly-buttered 8 inch (20cm) round tin and bake in a preheated oven at 180°C, 350°F, gas mark 4 for about an hour, or until the top is golden brown. Serve warm with whipped cream or custard.

Clotted Cream Cheesecake

Clotted cream is believed to have been introduced to the West Country by the Phoenicians who came to Cornwall in search of tin. Whatever its origin the rich yellow cream of Devon and the slightly thicker, more crusty, clotted cream of Cornwall are famous countrywide.

6 oz (170g) ginger biscuits, crushed
3 ½ oz (90g) melted butter
8 oz (225g) cream cheese
5 oz (125g) fromage frais
5 oz (125g) clotted cream
3 oz (75g) caster sugar
1 ½ oz (40g) cornflour
Grated rind and juice of a lemon
2 eggs
3 tbsp (45ml) sultanas

Put the biscuits in a plastic bag and crush with a rolling pin. Mix together in a bowl with the melted butter. Press the mixture into the base of an 8 inch (20cm) flan tin with a loose base. Put the cream cheese and fromage frais in a food processor and blend until smooth. Add the cream, sugar, cornflour, lemon rind and lemon juice, then blend in the eggs. Scatter the sultanas over the biscuit base, pour the filling on top and bake for 35 minutes at 180°C, 350°F , gas mark 4. Leave the cheesecake to cool completely before removing from the tin.

Walnut and Honey Tart

Walnuts used to grow in abundance in the West Country. This regional speciality combines with local honey in a deliciously rich dessert which should be served in small wedges with clotted cream.

3 oz (75g) butter or margarine, cut into small pieces
6 oz (170g) plain wholemeal flour
Finely grated rind and juice of an orange
4 tbsp (60ml) clear runny honey
3 oz (75g) fresh wholemeal breadcrumbs
3 tbsp (45ml) soft brown sugar
4 small eggs
4 oz (100g) chopped walnuts

In a mixing bowl rub the fat into the flour with your fingertips. Add the grated rind and sufficient juice to mix to a firm dough. Roll out on a lightly-floured board and use to line an 8 inch (20cm) diameter flan tin with a loose base. Bake blind for about 15 minutes in a preheated oven at 200°C, 400°F, gas mark 6. Mix the honey, breadcrumbs and brown sugar together, beat in the eggs one at a time, adding any remaining orange juice. Scatter the chopped walnuts on the bottom of the tart and pour over the honey mixture. Bake in a hot oven at 200°C, 400°F, gas mark 6 for about 25 minutes.

Helston Pudding

Dating from Saxon times, Helston's Furry or Floral Dance - a festival to usher in the summer - has been held every year on the 8 May. The Furry dancers, as they are known, are stylishly dressed: the men in top hats and morning coats, the ladies in long white gowns. They dance all through the town threading their way through the front door and out the back door of specially picked houses. The silver band plays and everyone sings the "Furry Song".

5 oz (125g) mixed dried fruit
2 oz (50g) shredded suet
2 oz (50g) caster sugar
2 oz (50g) breadcrumbs
2 oz (50g) ground rice
2 oz (50g) plain flour
1/2 teaspoon (2.5ml) mixed spice
1/2 teaspoon (2.5ml) bicarbonate of soda
Milk

In a large bowl mix together all the dry ingredients, except the soda. Dissolve the soda in a little of the milk and add this to the dry ingredients together with sufficient milk to mix into a stiff batter consistency. Pour into a well greased 1½ pint (900ml) basin, cover with two thicknesses of pleated greaseproof paper and steam for two hours.

Cider Syllabub

The "bub" in Syllabub is the Elizabethan slang word for sparkling wine. It was only in the nineteenth century that cider became a popular ingredient for this delicious dessert.

¾ pint (450ml) double cream
2 oz (50g) caster sugar
½ pint (300ml) sweet cider
1 tbsp (15ml) brandy or calvados
16 ratafia biscuits

Whip the cream until stiff. Gradually beat in the sugar and cider in a thin steady stream, then whisk in the brandy. The cream should be light and stiff enough to hold its shape. Place four ratafia biscuits in the bottom of four glass goblets, spoon the syllabub on top. Chill for at least an hour before serving.

Pickled Damsons

Pickled damsons are traditional to the West Country and are excellent served with coldmeats especially gammon.

3 lbs (1.5kg) damsons
1 pint (600ml) white wine vinegar
1½ lbs (675g) sugar
8 cloves and 1 stick cinnamon tied in muslin

Stone the damsons over a bowl so that any juice is saved. Add the vinegar and leave to stand overnight. Strain off the juice, and put the fruit into a clean bowl. Boil the juice and pour back over the fruit and leave for 24 hours. Put the fruit, juices, sugar and spices into a preserving pan, bring to the boil and cook for about 30 minutes. Remove the spice bundle and ladle the fruit into warmed clean jars. Seal and label.

Cornish Fairings

In medieval times a "maid-hiring" fair was held in the Cornish market town of Launceston. One of the great specialities on sale was the ginger-flavoured Cornish Fairings, cracked and golden brown in appearance.

4 oz (100g) plain flour
Good pinch of salt
1 tsp (5ml) bicarbonate of soda
1 tsp (5ml) baking powder
1 tsp (5ml) ground ginger
1 tsp (5ml) ground cinnamon
1 tsp (5ml) mixed spice
2 oz (50g) butter or margarine, cut into small pieces
2 oz (50g) caster sugar
2 tbsp (30ml) golden syrup

Makes 10

Sift the flour, salt, bicarbonate of soda, baking powder and spices into a large mixing bowl. Rub the fat into the flour mixture with the fingertips, until it resembles fine breadcrumbs. Stir in the sugar. In a small bowl over a pan of hot water, steam the golden syrup until runny. Add to the other ingredients and knead together. Roll the mixture into small balls and place on a greased baking tray, leaving space between each one. Bake at 200°C, 400°F, gas mark 6 at the top of the oven for about 10 minutes then move to the bottom of the oven for the last 5 minutes. Remove the biscuits with a spatula and cool on a wire rack.

Cornish Heavy Cake

This was a popular cake baked in Cornish fishing villages. Tradition has it that hearing the fishermen shouting "heave" as they pulled in the nets, their wives rushed to make a quick and easy cake for tea. Known locally as "Fuggan", the criss-cross pattern on the top of the cake is said to depict the fishing nets.

5 oz (125g) white pastry fat, cut into small pieces
1 lb (450g) plain flour
3 oz (75g) caster sugar
5 oz (125g) mixed dried fruit
½ pint (300ml) milk approximately
3 oz (75g) butter, cut into tiny pieces
1 small egg, beaten

In a mixing bowl rub the white pastry fat into the flour with the fingertips. Stir in the sugar, dried fruit and sufficient milk to make a stiff dough. On a floured board roll out to a long oblong. Dot with half the butter, then fold a third of the pastry in to the centre from both ends. Roll out again and repeat the buttering and folding. Criss-cross the top with a knife, brush with beaten egg and bake for 30 minutes at 190°C, 375°F, gas mark 5.

Saffron Cake

Introduced to Cornwall by the Spanish, saffron is the dried stigma of a purple flowering crocus, and up to the beginning of this century saffron crocuses were grown commercially in North Cornwall. Saffron adds colour and a unique flavour to this cake.

Good pinch of saffron strands
1 oz (25g) fresh yeast
¼ pint (150ml) warm milk
1 lb (450g) strong plain flour
1 tsp (5ml) salt
4 oz (100g) butter, cut into small pieces
6 oz (170g) dried mixed fruit
Grated rind of half an orange
1 oz (25g) caster sugar

Put the saffron strands into a bowl and cover with ¼ pint (150ml) boiling water and leave to stand overnight. Blend the yeast with the milk and let stand in a warm place for about 20 minutes. Rub the flour, salt and butter together until the mixture resembles fine breadcrumbs. Stir in the mixed fruit, orange rind and sugar. Strain the saffron, put the liquid into a pan and warm, then pour over the other ingredients. Stir in the milk and yeast mixture and beat well. Turn the dough into a greased 8-inch (20cm) cake tin, cover and let stand in a warm place for about an hour. When the mixture has risen to almost the top of the tin, bake for 30 minutes at 200°C, 400°F, gas mark 6 then reduce the heat to 180°C, 350°F, gas mark 4 for a further 30 minutes.

This spicy cake dates back to the eighteenth century.

1 lb (450g) plain flour
½ tsp (2.5ml) bicarbonate of soda
4 oz (100g) butter, cut into small pieces
2 tsp (10ml) ground cinnamon
1 lb (450g) currants
8 oz (225g) chopped crystallised ginger
4 oz (100g) mixed chopped peel
2 eggs
5 fl oz (130ml) warm milk

Sift the flour and bicarbonate of soda together in a large mixing bowl, add the butter and rub into the flour. Stir in the cinnamon, currants, crystallised ginger and mixed peel. Beat the eggs and add to the bowl with sufficient milk to mix to a soft dough. Spoon into a lightly greased 9 inch (23cm) cake tin and bake for two hours at 180°C, 350°F, gas mark 4.

Brandy Butter

Brandy first came into England in the seventeenth century and quickly became very popular. When shipwrecks occurred along the treacherous shores of the South West any stray barrels of brandy were quickly seized and hidden out of sight of the Customs men.

4 oz (100g) unsalted softened butter
2 tbsp (30ml) caster sugar
4 tbsp (60ml) brandy

Cream the butter and sugar together until nice and fluffy. Beat in the brandy a few drops at a time, beating well between each addition, until the brandy has all been absorbed into the butter. Serve with Christmas Pudding, mince pies or any steamed pudding.

Wassail Cup

Throughout the West Country, and especially in Somerset's cider apple orchards, the old custom of wassailing the fruit trees to encourage fertility and growth is still practiced. The Wassail Bowl is passed around and drunk by everybody assembled around the trees. This old custom was described by Robert Herrick in 1648 thus:

> Wassaile the trees that they might beare
> You many a plum and many a peare;
> For more or lesse fruits they will bring
> As you do give them wassailing.

3 small dessert apples
3 oz (75g) soft dark brown sugar
2 pints (1.1 litre) brown ale
½ pint (300ml) dry sherry
½ tsp (2.5ml) each of ground cinnamon, nutmeg and ginger
Zest of half a lemon

Score the skin of each apple around its middle and put in a large cast iron casserole dish. Sprinkle over the brown sugar and about 4 tablespoons of the brown ale. Cover and bake for about 20 minutes at 190°C, 375°F, gas mark 5. Take the apples out of the dish and add the remaining brown ale, sherry, spices and lemon peel and simmer on a low heat for 5 minutes. Return the apples to the dish and serve at once.

WEST COUNTRY COOKBOOK

Index of Recipes

Appletree Press